THE ~~FRUSTRATED~~ CONCERNED HR

A SUCCESS GUIDE FOR CAREER AND LIFE

Stacy-Ann M Nelson

2020

THE PUBLISHER'S
NOTEBOOK LIMITED
"ENVISION IT. WE'LL PUBLISH IT"

Dedication

We all have people who motivate and believe in us. I am blessed to have that support, and I dedicate this book to them.

I dedicate this book to my parents, Cecil & Dothlyn Nelson, my siblings Carlotta, Oliver, Fitzroy, La-Shawn and my sister-in-law Tenneisha. I also dedicate this book to the loves of my life, my nieces and nephews; Anton, Javoun, Bianca, Danielle, Ajani, Naila and Micah.

I am who I am because of them, and I love them all endlessly.

To the memory of my friend Faylin, now deceased. I am sad that she is not here to see the fruit, but I remain thankful that she truly believed in me. She was confident that I am a writer and that I will walk in this purpose! This book is also dedicated to her.

Table of Contents

Preface i

Acknowledgements iv

Introduction vi

Resume and Curriculum Vitae – What is the difference? 1

Preparing the Package 26

Attitude- Your vehicle of advancement or instrument of demise 33

Getting Ready for your Future Career 42

Preparing to Hunt 46

Choose a Career and not a Job 52

Who are your friends? 57

Do not live in a state of someday 63

You better tear those muscles! 69

Faith it until you Make It! 74

Swimming with the sharks 78

How to know if this is YOUR job 84

Make your last waltz your best waltz 88

Go the 40th time! 92

About Stacy-Ann M. Nelson 96

Preface

From the age of twenty-three years old, I embarked on a career path of impacting the lives of people, from newborn to ninety-nine years old by becoming a Social Worker. At age thirty-one years old, I started my career as a Human Resource Professional, still on the path of impacting people's lives.

For eighteen years, I have made many behavioural and social observations, counselled many people on their personal and professional lives, interviewed hundreds of candidates from Senior Management to ancillary, and have supervised many people, directly and indirectly.

Throughout my career, I have had a great vantage point from which to observe people. I have seen many succeed, I have seen some struggle, and I have seen many failures. My years of experience have stirred and aggravated me to feel a responsibility to help. My goal is to help people to understand that they determine the outcome of their lives. Therefore, they must take ownership of their lives, think bigger than their present state, and realize that they have a greater value than what they have settled for. This desire evolved through my personal introspection that revealed I was also operating in a space of comfort and stagnation.

I have interviewed people and left the interviews feeling distressed and extremely concerned that so many people need help putting their "package" together. The untidiness of their "packages" was causing them to fail at shining in the presence of a panel of people looking to hire the best.

This book is for me, and for you.

I am making use of my God given talent to walk into my purpose of being a helper.

It is a book prepared from a place of love and strong desire to empower you with knowledge, encourage you to push yourself beyond imagined limits, improve your odds of acquiring the job you desire, to truly launch your career or become a great entrepreneur. This book is for anyone at any age, and at any stage in their career.

It is also an amalgamation of professional and life advice. You will enjoy the nuggets and life lessons that will shift your mind and give you clarity on life while you sharpen your focus on achieving your goals. There is no time like the present to take a step towards better, and I guarantee you that reading this book is a step towards better.

The time is now, seize the growth moments!

Acknowledgements

As the song says, "No man is an island, no man stands alone". To achieve any measure of success, we all need a support system, and I thank God I know and have experienced mine. Embarking on my maiden book voyage, I was supported and encouraged, and I must acknowledge the people who made this book possible.

First and foremost, I must acknowledge the King of Kings and Lord of Lords, Jesus Christ. The Bible says that ***"We can do all things through Christ who strengthens us"*** (Philippians 4:13) and this is indeed true. God has, through the Holy Spirit, filled me with knowledge, confidence and the desire to walk in purpose. I could not have finished writing this book without His undergirding. Glory to God.

My "tita" (sister) La-Shawn, was a tower of strength and motivation. Her belief in me and my abilities, was a true confidence booster. She kept me accountable and cheered me on. La-Shawn, thank you.

Layla aka Lala, my friend for over twenty years for her unwavering confidence in my abilities and continuous support.

The Sisterhood, my group of professional female friends who are boss ladies - Melissa, Shereen, Diana, Diane, Rhona, Shaniel, Alisha, Jasmine and Sandrice.

My Pastor, Bishop McLean. You agitate me to be better and walk in purpose and this book is a fruit of your teaching.

My Editor and Publisher, Sylvia Dallas of The Publisher's Notebook Ltd - a resounding thank you! Your genuine interest in ensuring the quality of the book was felt and appreciated. You are insightful, professional and extremely talented at what you do. This book would not have come to light without you.

Introduction

"Be who you were created to be, and you will set the world on fire"

- St. Catherine of Sienna

The quote above may be simplistic in its construction, but powerful in meaning. From an early age, I was always concerned about my life. That is, *what will I become, what life will I live* and as I grew older, I added *how will I impact people*. If we care to admit, many of us spent years living our lives in a state of mediocrity, and not presenting ourselves in the best packages. We lose opportunities as a result of poor self-branding.

Unhappiness, unfulfillment, regret, failures, and disappointments all flow from the same stream. That is the stream of lack of preparation mixed with fear. When we fail to plan, opportunities arise and we are ill-prepared thus losing the chances. Fear creeps in with thoughts of not being good enough, fear of rejection, and even fear of excelling.

Happiness, success, newness, walking in purpose and self-fulfillment flow from the stream of preparation, taking a chance, and leaping in faith to do that which you have always wanted to do.

This book is not written to convince you to leave your job or go explore entrepreneurship. As you invest your time reading this book, it will provide you with the tools to equip you to improve your personal brand and do better as you develop in your career and life at any stage. Each chapter is a developmental guide that encourages you to go deep diving in self, excavating what is deep within - talents, habits, and passions. It is a challenge to take a chance on you by being willing to improve how you market yourself, to stop settling, be more mindful of your companions by being careful about choosing your circle of friends and extending your network.

All the knowledge in the world and a great group of friends or network, cannot compensate for a great attitude. Knowledge and connections may open doors for you, but a good attitude will keep the doors open and open many more doors. Conversely, a poor attitude will close those once open doors, and keep you from entering through doors of greater opportunities. As you explore the pages of this book, you will gain great insight into key soft skills that are critical to your success in not just career, but your entire life. You will also be nourished with incredible understanding of how to navigate through your workspaces, and gain the most from these experiences, rather than being swallowed by situations and people you will inevitably meet.

It was important for me to include a chapter on managing relations with people because of experiences I have had particularly on my very first "real" job at about age 20 or 21 years old. The Operations Manager took a real dislike to me, as she assumed her once paramour was sweet on me. You see, this man was a top executive wielding a lot of power. He did in fact take a liking to me, but I certainly did not reciprocate. In fact one day he said to me, "you are dangerous because you are so seductive and don't even know it". Because she perceived it would be hard to resist a man with such power, I guess she assumed I fell in the web. When I resigned, I was not leaving the job because of her entirely (but partly), but on my last day there, I received one of the best advices to date! A very reserved but observant older lady saw me in the restroom and said, "Stacy, wherever you go there will be Mrs. Blacks (name changed to protect privacy), but it is how you deal with the Mrs. Blacks that will make a difference". The chapter on "Swimming with the sharks" was inspired by that advice though it took me some years to truly get it. My prayer and hope is that after reading that chapter, you will be very equipped to dive in the "dangerous deep blue" and be just fine.

All the chapters are laced with nuggets that are beneficial and critical for you at all stages of your adult life and career. "Adulting" is not easy and we all need assistance as we navigate. As you embark on your careers and face challenges, hiccups and red lights at various stages, I have encased sound resource in this book to help you along the way.

Let your excitement to be the best you lead you. As I leave you with this book, I am right there on every page you turn cheering you on and guiding you along. The exercises within are there to get you thinking and acting and you will be the better for doing them.

You are now just one page away from transformation. TURN TO IT!

Chapter One

Resume and Curriculum Vitae – What is the difference?

Before explaining the differences, let us discuss the similarity. Resumes and curriculum vitae are both introductory tools used by job seekers to introduce themselves to a recruiter or prospective employer. They are personal marketing documents.

Curriculum Vitae

A curriculum vitae is credential based. It is a concise representation of your experiences and skills. It is generally two pages long or more, depending on the extent of the candidate's accomplishments. A curriculum vitae includes information such as academic background, teaching experiences, research, publications, licenses, professional associations and notable awards, considered relevant to the position of interest to the candidate.

Based on the extent of the candidate's experience and accomplishments, a curriculum vitae may be longer than a resume. A curriculum vitae is a pointed tool used to quickly sum up and precisely and concisely communicate a candidate's experiences and skills.

Resume

Resumes are relatively more popularly known and used by job seekers. Resumes are written presentation of one's education, work history, and credentials. Resumes generally have an objective or career summary statement. A word to the wise, do not let the words of your objective or career summary statement be arbitrary. Spend time thinking about it and align it to the job for which you are applying. Typically, your resume should be one page (take out the unnecessary fluff).

Whether you choose a resume or a curriculum vitae, you must ensure that this introductory visual presentation of you, to be received by recruiters and prospective employers is a good one. It will decide whether you receive or not receive an invitation to be interviewed for the job in which you have interest.

The Purpose of a Resume

A resume is much more than a description of your educational background, work experiences and skills. It is your introductory tool to a recruiter or future employer. It is the first impression of who you are; it is your representative.

It is also that document that highlights your background and education. It showcases your skills, competencies and tells the story of your successes and achievements. Therefore, how you present yourself on your resume determines whether a door opens for you to step in or remains close.

The Format of Your Resume

The format or presentation of your resume should be determined by the following:

- o If you are a recent graduate

- o A skilled or semi-skilled person

- o An aspiring leader/manager

- o A seasoned leader/manager

What is critical for your resume?

Recent Graduate

- Apart from stating the discipline of your Degree, Certificate or Diploma, it is vital to list completed courses that are pertinent to the position for which you are applying. This is not to say you must list all your courses. Rather, you must highlight the courses that equipped you with the theoretical and practical knowledge, to perform the responsibilities required of the desired incumbent the company is seeking. Therefore, while you may not have the requisite on the job experiences, highlighting your exposure to the relevant areas coupled with other critical skills can "pry the door open". Providing this background information communicates that you have the foundational knowledge to accelerate you around the learner curve.

- Highlight your achievements and academic recognitions. It communicates that you are an achiever, one who gets result. To the students reading this book I pause here to underscore to you the importance of going hard, putting in the extra work to get more than the pass grade and to aim for excellence.

- Highlight extracurricular activities, societies and clubs in which you were involved and any positions of leadership responsibilities you held. These communicate that you possess team working skills and leadership abilities.

- Include summer jobs, internships or voluntary activities on your resume. By doing this you are sharing that you have been exposed to the world of work and thus should have some understanding of what is expected in terms of code of conduct in a professional environment.

<u>Skilled or Semi- Skilled</u>

- It is fundamental that your resume lucidly expresses what you have done with your skills. If you are a Web Designer, highlight some of the outstanding designs you created. Your accomplishments are more important than a chronological regurgitation of your job description. You resume must be evidence based.

<u>Aspiring Leader/Manager -</u>

- If you have aspirations for, but have never held a leadership role, start by volunteering when the opportunity arises. Requesting to be a part of a project committee or, organizing lunch and learn sessions are examples of some of the pursuits that will demonstrate your zeal. These kinds of activities not only build your resume but expose you to some leadership roles. This also allows you to determine the leadership style and traits that you need to develop.

- You are laying the foundation for your platform of leadership. Therefore, when you put on your resume that you were the chairperson for committees, or lead your team to achieve particular goals, you can refer to it in an interview. Before the door even opens, having them on your resume says, "I have leadership potential and I have used this potential to some extent." Some typical questions are:

    o What experience have you had that you believe has prepared you for this management or supervisory role?

    o What challenges have you had as a leader?

    o Describe your leadership style?

    o How do you handle conflicts among team members?

    o Tell of a problem you faced while executing your job? Do not just focus on the problem itself, tell them how you resolved it.

<u>Seasoned Leader -</u>

- As a seasoned leader with more than five years' experience in leadership roles, your resume must speak to the hard things – quantifiable achievements. Your resume must articulate how you have grown your division or department, and by extension the company. Your resume should detail:

    o What you have implemented

    o Committees you have led

    o Leadership societies or groups to which you belong

    o As a seasoned leader, your resume must indicate action and results.

If you are in a leadership position but you do not have the latitude to do a lot, create your own opportunities. Offer your assistance in other areas of the company, sit on committees, initiate projects in areas where you assess the need for such and overall be willing and open to extend yourself. When your resume is coloured with these experiences, it communicates flexibility, open-mindedness and adaptability.

Resume Dos and Don'ts

When a job is advertised, remember you are not the only person who has seen the advertisement, neither will you be the only person applying for it. Depending on the job, and the job market at the time, hundreds may apply. All those other applicants are your competitors in the race for the prize. You must now consider how you are going to distinguish yourself, ensure your resume gets in and score you an interview. You must employ your best marketing strategy.

Below is a table of some "dos and don'ts" for you to consider when putting together your "marketing proposal" – your resume.

Do's	DON'Ts
Use a style that is clean and not too busy. Use easy to read font.	Do not clutter your resume with unnecessary information. Age is not required, Date of Birth, neither your address nor marital status.
Keep your resume short and to the point. No more than two pages maximum. Quality over quantity.	Do not submit a booklet. It won't be read.
Be truthful about what you	If you don't know it, don't

Do's	DON'Ts
write.	claim it. Do not embellish or lie. If you don't have mastery don't say you do. Remember you will have to prove it.
Spell and grammar check.	Do not submit resume with spelling and grammatical errors.
Tailor your resume for the job. Look at the job for which you are applying, and tailor your resume to show what is necessary for the job description.	Do not do a one size fits all resume.
Use active voice in your resume. E.g. I managed the implementation of the new software.	Do not use passive voice, it comes across disingenuous. E.g. The implementation of the new software was managed by me.
Use power verbs and action words for bulleted points.	Don't use first person pronouns "I, me, we" – not professional.
Include personal accomplishments that show off some skills you have (technical and soft), awards you have won, recognition	Quit including these genetic hobbies; reading, watching television or surfing the internet. No one cares because they are

Do's	DON'Ts
for some work, published articles etc.	irrelevant and are quite frankly, juvenile. If not transferrable to work, it's not important to be there.
Consider a Professional Summary Statement. This should be brief and encapsulate you as a professional with accomplishments.	Do not include objective statements. Objectives are only necessary if you are making a change in career.
Create and use a professional email address.	Do not use a personal email address that suggests frivolous, flirtatious or raunchy behaviour.

Objectives or Professional Statement?

An *objective* speaks to what you want, while a *professional statement* describes who you are and what you are about. The tone must be strong or confident and positive. In a very concise way (no more than three or four sentences in a paragraph) highlight relevant skills, and experiences. It should clearly state who you are professionally and what they (the company) stand to benefit from based on your experiences and ambitions.

<u>**Basics to remember**</u>

- Be mindful of the font and font sizes used. Your name must be the biggest font size on your resume. It communicates confidence.

- Resume style (If a graphics or IT savvy person you want to reflect that)

- Grammar – use proper grammar and tenses. Read over and get someone to proofread your work. You may also utilize modern technology such as Grammarly.

<u>**Sample adjectives to use**</u>

Below are some sample action words:

- Lead

- Organized

- Implemented

- Designed

- Developed

- Co-ordinated

- Spearheaded

<u>Cover Letter</u>

A nicely evenly toasted slice of bread is good, but what makes the toast even better is a lathering of butter over the warm bread. Your cover letter should be that butter to your resume – the warm slice of toast.

Your resume details your accomplishments on the job, academically and socially. The cover letter goes as a complimentary document, not a duplicate of the resume. It is that document that gives that critical first impression of you to the recruiter or potential employer.

Purposes of your Cover Letter

1. To explain your interest in the position and working with the particular company.

2. To state the specific skills and knowledge you possess that makes you ideal for the job.

3. To communicate what makes you suitable for the organization, that is, why you believe you are not just fit for the job but fit for the company also.

4. To give evidence or example of instances where you excelled in a particular area(s) that

were mentioned in the job description for the job you are applying for.

Your cover letter should be succinct. There is no need to write a long epistle filled with repetition as some people often do.

Important parts of a letter

A cover letter must have the following:

a) **Heading**: This should be at the top of the letter. It includes your name and contact information such as telephone number and email.

b) **Date**: This is the date you prepared the letter.

c) **Inside Address**: This should start with the name of the person to whom you are writing, their job title, name of the company and then the company's address.

d) **Salutation/Greeting**: Ensure you use proper designations; Mr., Miss, Mrs., Dr., etc.

e) **Opening Paragraph/Introduction**: State in this paragraph how you became aware of the job and your reason for applying. State convincingly why you have interest in the job.

f) **Second paragraph**: This is your sales pitch. In this paragraph you write briefly about your qualifications being careful not to detail what is already on your resume. Highlight achievements that are relatable to the job being applied for. This is critical in presenting yourself as a suitable candidate. Also add information about your soft skills that are relevant to the position.

g) **Closing Paragraph**: Re-emphasize your interest in working with the company and state your availability to meet. Also, in this paragraph make mention of your accompanying resume.

h) **Complimentary Closing** that is often Regards or Sincerely.

i) **Signature Line**: If sending online, you should add your electronic signature.

Cover Letter Do's and Don'ts

Do's	DON'Ts
Tailor made – make it specific to the job/position being applied for.	Don't recycle your cover letters for various jobs.

Do's	DON'Ts
Market your skills and personal attributes that match what the prospective employer needs for the job.	Do not make it a duplication of your resume.
Use action verbs and phrases.	Do not beg for the job. Avoid pleading or stating how desperate you are for a job.
Use confident but not arrogant language.	Do not use slangs or colloquial terms.
Be original in your writing.	Do not use coloured or perfumed papers.
Use industry jargons.	Do not use "fancy" fonts that may be difficult to read.
Use proper grammar and punctuations.	Do not send your letter unsigned.
Proofread and also have someone proofread for you.	Do not copy a document from the internet and use as your own.
Be specific in referencing relevant achievements.	Do not be afraid to ask for assistance in proof reading.
Identify key words used in the advertisement and incorporate them. Example – Core Values – In highlighting your soft skills speak to at least two	Do not re-write the advertisement.

Do's	DON'Ts
attributes that you know you exemplify.	
Keep your cover letter on one page.	Do not write an essay.

An ugly, unkempt package will often be left untouched even if there is an expensive gift on the inside. Presentation is important. You may be the best person for the job but how you present yourself on paper will determine if you get the opportunity to let the recruiter know how superb you are. Take time to prepare that cover letter; remember, it is the butter to your toast.

Interviews

The keys to acing an interview are:

- o Preparation

- o Having a presence (dress & speech)

- o Transparency and honesty

Preparation: If you are going into an interview without preparing, as the saying goes, you are preparing to fail. Know this, preparation invites and attracts success. You must be prepared to do the following:

- Answer questions about the industry and position you applied for. If asked about what you know about the company and the latest happens in the industry and you cannot answer, it communicates laziness, disinterest and really that you are not prepared or serious about working with the company or in the industry. This is a bonus question so research, research and research.

- You must have your "elevator response" to common get to know you interview questions. Tell us about yourself? Why do you believe you are ideal for this job? What value will you bring to the position? If you describe yourself using some key adjectives, be prepared to expound – give example(s) of how you demonstrated dedication, problem-solving, lateral thinking and so on. Your elevator response or pitch as some call it, is your advertisement. It is your succinct speech that must communicate essential information about you to your interviewers indicating how you will be of value to the organization.

- Anticipate possible concerns the interviewers may have about you or your experiences and prepare your responses. For example, if it's a new job or new industry that you have never worked in, the interviewer may express concern about that. Be prepared to allay concerns by speaking about your willingness to learn, how flexible you are, and how transferable your skills and competencies are regardless of the industry. If you have examples of how you seamlessly transitioned before, speak about them. Additionally, if you are seeking a supervisory or management job without prior experiences, speak on how you have been prepared, talk about various leadership experiences, refer to any example you have of stepping into leadership roles by assisting colleagues.

Presence: Your posture and gait in an interview are areas that can cause you to gain or lose points with the interviewer. Here are some points to gain points:

- Make eye contact. Inability to make eye contact and hold it without being weird about it is important. Being able to make eye contact with interviewers makes you appear sincere, genuine, and professional and says you are focused and interested. Experts have said that when speaking to people and they are looking away, it communicates that the person is uncomfortable, lacks self-confidence, or may be lying. When making eye contact in interviews let your eyes "smile" in a professional manner, of course.

- Do not speak with your hands. Gesticulating is distracting and will be off-putting to interviewers. If you are interviewing around a conference table, keep your hands steady (being careful not to "strangle" the desk). You may slightly clasp your fingers or put one hand over the other to keep them down. If there is no desk, place your hands in your lap or lightly on your knees. Do not cross your arms.

Whether around a desk or not, do not sit and swing the chair or tap your feet on the ground or tap your fingers on the desk.

- Do not ramble. Listen to the question asked, think about your response then vocalize the response. Taking a few seconds to think is perfectly acceptable. If for any reason you did not quite comprehend what was asked, you may repeat the question aloud, and politely ask if your understanding of the question is correct. Do not say, "eehh, go again" or any other colloquial slangs you may be accustomed to using with friends.

- Score success early. Interviewers generally sum up a candidate in the first five minutes of the interview. When you enter the room bring energy (not so much that you appear fake or under the influence of some substance), enthusiasm and politeness. Shake the hands of the interviewers and thank them for inviting you (it is okay to do this at the beginning). If the interviewers are entering a room where you are already seated, stand and greet them with a smile and handshake. Your warmth opens them up to hear from you, especially if they were interviewing other candidates before you.

- Take a copy of your resume. Also walk with a portfolio to show your work if that is at all possible. It allows the interviewer to see what you have done and provides an opportunity for you to talk about what you can do and have done.

- Have questions prepared to ask the interviewers. **NEVER** say you have no questions. Also, construct and ask questions that are relevant and sensible. You may want to ask what are the key deliverables you will be expected to achieve in the first six months on the job, ask about the company's culture, ask about the company's immediate and long term strategic goals, the structure of the department to which you will belong if successful, and if the company is involved in any social activities are some of the basic questions you may ask.

Your interview may begin from you enter the compound – **MIND YOUR MANNERS AND DISPOSITION** while waiting to be interviewed. Be courteous to everyone, this includes the parking attendant or security guard. If you make or receive a telephone call while waiting, keep it brief and professional in tone. Even if the interviewers are running late and you are annoyed, do not show it whether through body language or facial expressions. Refrain from hissing your teeth. Sit quietly and wait or read a magazine or newspaper that may be available. Also be observant. Take note of the company's mission and vision statements, and core values that may be on display in the waiting area or boardroom where you are seated, and you can most definitely ask questions in relation to them when given the opportunity to ask your questions. Of course, while waiting, you may discreetly review your interview notes. Do not appear to be swatting.

While the interviewer may be allowed to be late you are not afforded that privilege. Ensure you get to the interview at least fifteen minutes early. This allows you time to compose yourself, relax, review your notes and observe the environment to somewhat assess the temperature and culture of the organization. Also, lateness in getting to the interview scores negatively against you.

Be positive. Go in thinking you have something great to offer the company and communicate your worth.

End on a good note by thanking the interviewer(s) for giving you the opportunity to share with them your knowledge and skills. End with a firm handshake and look into the eyes of the interviewers as you shake their hands. When you get up from the chair, fix it back properly under the table and don't leave it twisted. It really says something about your persona – unpolished.

Please do not speak of or make reference to yourself in the third person. Doing so is simply weird and creepy.

When asked direct questions regarding anything you accomplished on your last job, do not answer by talking about "we". If it is in relation to what you have done, speak about you. By saying "we" it gives the impression that you are less than genuine and that perhaps you did not do as you claim.

Drop the over familiarity and slangs. When in an interview, your posture and speech must be totally professional and delicately balanced with warmth and being engaging. Do not refer to interviewers as, "you people", or "you guys".

Thank you. Always send a thank you email. Keep it brief. Just express your appreciation for the interview and put final punch regarding your excitement about the job and company and how you can add value (be specific regarding the value you bring to the table).

Interviews continue until you leave the compound. Do not drop your guard after exiting the room with interviewers. Do not hiss your teeth, frown, quick to take out our cell phone to call a friend and vent or make sarcastic comments. When leaving, remember employees may be in earshot, cameras may still be on you or the receptionist may be asked to evaluate your post interview posture and report to the interviewers.

This is not just for interviews but basic professional etiquette – the chewing of gum is an **absolute no**. If you were chewing gum prior to the interview, take out the gum before entering the room with the interviewers.

You will not be taking a call during your interview so no need to hold your phone in your hand or rest it on the boardroom table. Make sure it is placed on silent before entering.

After your resume opens the door, the interview is the way you seal the deal. Your interview is your moment in the spotlight, it is your time to shine or go dim. So prepare, have a winning and engaging presence and be sincere. A great and experienced interviewer has the ability to sum you up in a few minutes.

Chapter Two

Preparing the Package

The Package is **you**. It is your look, your attitude, your speech, your skills and talents. Whether we wish to admit it or not, we are highly visual people. We like to have our eyes tantalized/titillated. In Jamaica, there is a saying "titivate". We say people love to titivate (fix up). Think about two gifts being presented to you; one wrapped with fancy paper, decorated with a neatly tied bow and have a nice greeting card. The other is crushed wrapped in obviously used brown paper, a bit soiled and tattered looking.

You are most likely set your eyes lustfully on the neat pretty package and scoff at the tattered one before you even open it, even though the better gift might be in the ugly package. Why is this being referenced? Presentation is important. Do not let the interviewer's natural inclination to shut out the scruffy happen to you. People can be turned off by how you present yourself that they do not even give you a fair chance.

You must be very intentional about the first impression you make, and your attire is one deciding factor of the first impression you give that will make or break the opportunity. Remember, a person's impression of you is partly formed by how you present yourself. Industries, organization cultures and locations impact the company's expectations of how candidates and employees must dress. What is standard however, is that candidates are expected to be well groomed, and clean.

There are some distinct differences between how one dresses for a formal or business casual interview.

Formal Interviews

Formal interviews are generally for corporate positions or office positions.

Men interview attire

- Men should wear a well fitted long sleeved shirt that is properly ironed. White is always a safe and good choice though not a requirement. The shirt should be paired with a clean simple (not busy patterned) tie; a solid would be good. Pants of a dark colour should be worn preferably navy, black or brown. The pants should also be ironed and stain or soil free. Also, wear a sleek leather belt, no oversized buckle.

- Limit the amount of jewelry you wear. A nice watch and one ring are adequate. Do not wear a watch that is too big as this will clatter on the boardroom table if or when you move your hands. While it is acceptable that you want to smell good, go easy on the aftershave and cologne. Overpowering scents may be overpowering and a turn-off for interviewers. On a more serious side, an interviewer may have an allergic response to the strong scents.

- Grooming of your hair is very important. Ensure you shave and cut your hair. Research the company to ascertain how conservative they are, so you do not go to the interview with your hair groomed in any way that may be scoffed at. While personal style and freedom of expression through style is understandable, just know that how you choose to express yourself through your style, may be contrary to the grooming policy of the company to which, you are seeking to be employed. If you have locks, ensure you have it freshly washed and groomed. Additionally, have your nails clean and trimmed.

Women interview attire

- Though unfair, what a woman wears attracts more judgement than a man. Therefore, women have much more to consider when preparing their interview attire.

- *Dress:* If wearing a dress, it should be of a dark colour. If not dark, it should not be too bright in colour. If it happens to be sleeveless, pair it with a coordinated blazer. While there is no rule that stockings must be worn with a dress or skirt, it certainly polishes out your look for an interview so go ahead and wear a pair.

- *Suits:* A well-tailored pants or skirt suit says, "I am here for business and I am not playing around". If opting for a pants suit, make sure the pants is well fitted but not so tight that it leaves nothing to the imagination!

- *Skirts*: Skirt length is important. A very short skirt says, "I am thirsty and will do anything for this job". An extra-long skirt might say, "I am very conservative and rigid". Skirts should be no more than two inches above or below the knees.

- *Hairstyles:* Your hair can be neat and nicely styled without being flashy. Whether you wear natural, processed, or "purchased hair", the one rule is to not let your hairstyle grab the attention. Again, know the company and groom your hair accordingly if you are serious about gaining employment there.

- *Nails and Polish*: Ensure your nails are groomed and clean. Have them at a modest length and keep the nail polish or nail art calm. Do not let your nails make a louder statement than you.

- *Perfume*: Certainly, smell good, but when wearing fragrance be mindful not to wear those that are overpowering in order not to aggravate or trigger allergies. I have been in interviews with candidates whose perfumes were so overpowering that I just could not get pass the smell to really interview the candidate, so this is real. Take heed.

- Shoes: These are generally statement pieces for both men and women. While your shoes are often an extension of your persona, ensure they are appropriate. No heavy platform stilettoes just a sensible heel will do for the interview.

Business Casual Interviews

Some companies are more business casual. When interviewing with such companies the formal suit is not necessary.

- **Men:** Men might opt to wear a cotton button-up shirt with slacks or dark wash jeans (blue or black). A blazer may also be added for a little extra to the outfit. With a blazer, he may wear a neatly fitted polo shirt with slacks or dark jeans. Men may also wear a vest or cardigan. A decent belt and clean shoes are still required, likewise all other grooming rules still holds.

- **Women:** Females may wear a dress (stocking not required) or button-up cotton shirt with a skirt or pants. Women may opt to polish up the look a bit more by adding a blazer or cardigan. All basic grooming requirements are still relevant.

It is important to mention here that although the company's culture may be laid back or casual, one still must endeavour to make a good first impression.

Personal Hygiene: Personal Hygiene is critical. If you suffer from halitosis, make sure you pay special attention to brushing your teeth and tongue and drink water to keep your mouth from being hot and dry. Also, walk with some mouthwash and if you have time before the interview, visit the restroom and discreetly give a good swoosh of mouthwash before the interview. You may also use breath fresher spray or lozenges. Do not go into the interview chewing gum to keep your mouth fresh.

Managerial Candidates

If you are seeking a managerial position, I say step it up a notch and wear a suit preferably a dark coloured suit with a complimenting shirt and tie. For female managerial candidates, wear a power pants or skirt suit of a dark colour.

Whether male or female, ensure the suit is tailored and fits you well. An ill-fitted frumpy suit does not make you look business like.

Chapter Three

Attitude- Your vehicle of advancement or instrument of demise

How you dress, look and act is your business card. Each must be diligently crafted and refined to open doors for you as the well-known adage says, "Your attitude determines your altitude". It is true that people make assumptions and form impressions of you just by seeing you; however, you cannot dress up a bad attitude. It shows up despite how clean, neat or fancy your clothes may be. Attitude opens doors and shuts doors. You may train people for a job but you can't train them for a good attitude.

Soft and Hard Skills

There are two types of skills that are imperative for candidates to possess soft and hard skills. To be successful at interviews, candidates must put both on display.

Hard Skills

- Hard skills are teachable abilities or skill sets. These are the quantifiable set of skills that are required for a job and are usually included in job postings and job descriptions.

- Hard skills are acquired through formal education and training. To be a medical doctor, you must know human anatomy – hard skill. A Construction or Mechanical Engineer must know Physics - hard skill and to be an Accountant, you must know accounting principles – hard skills.

- To sell your hard skills or rather convince the interviewers that you possess the competencies, you must be able to effectively answer job specific questions. Prepare for this by studying the job and advertisement to become familiar with exactly what the incumbent will be required to deliver. Additionally, when given the opportunity to ask questions, it is a great time to ask impressive questions relating to the job, to let the interviewer know you understand what the job entails.

- Unfortunately, some underestimate the value of soft skills. Soft skills are those competencies that determine whether you will truly be a rounded success in your job. Soft skills are "people skills" or "interpersonal skills". These set of skills determine your work ethic, whether you will be respected or liked or be of influence. Soft skills are formed from the core of who you are, that is, your character.

- Soft skills include your communication, leadership, teamwork, time management, work ethic, motivation and problem-solving abilities. Your soft skills determine your attitude towards your job, your colleagues and your supervisors and leaders.

- Unlike hard skills, soft skills are not easily detected in an interview and are unquantifiable. To assess the soft skills that are deemed necessary for a job, the interviewer will ask questions relating to past behaviours. You may be asked to explain how you handled such and such situation in the past. The interviewers are seeking to analyse your response to situations, which gives them insight to your soft skills. Not only will they ask questions to probe what you did, they will ask situational questions to assess how you will handle situations.

Some prospective employers employ Psychometric Testing or Personality Profile Assessment Tools to discover a candidate's soft skills. A research conducted by the Society of Human Resource Management (SHRM) found that employers care more about soft skills than they do technical abilities like reading, comprehension and mathematics.

According to one Kathy Robinson of Turning Point, "Soft skills are keys to building relationships, gaining visibility, and creating more opportunities for advancement".

In demand soft skills

- **Communication**: This is both written and verbal communication. Communication facilitates your interaction with others and largely determines their impressions of you. It is important to be mindful of your oral and written tone as these send messages and can be received positively or negatively. In oral or verbal communication, master confident but not arrogant tone. Speak clearly and fluently to command attention, hold the audience and be interesting. You must also learn how to use your tone to communicate empathy. When writing, choose your words carefully, proofread to minimize errors and be precise and to the point.

Effective communicators are valued by an organization because they are generally productive good leaders and simply, make work less dramatic and complicated. They facilitate good work relations.

How to harvest your communication skills? Practice makes perfect. Practice your presentation skills, tape and listen to yourself, join your local Toastmasters or even watch videos on how to improve your communication.

- **Ability to work in a team**: Even if the job does not necessarily require you to always work in a team, teamwork is essential for the accomplishing of company goals. A company's success is achieved through the efforts of more than one person working towards mutual goals. To be a great team player you must appreciate the role each person plays on the team and in the company, be willing to extend yourself beyond your desk or your job, be dependable and do all you do to the best of your ability. Employers are looking for people who are collaborators, extra-milers and people who are willing to jump in and help others "row the boat".

- **Problem Solving**: Some people are problem finders and complainers and some people see the problems and find solutions. Which of the two would you consider to be more valuable to an organization? Certainly, it is the latter. To be a top performer, you must naturally possess or develop the ability to find solutions to problematic situations. Companies are seeking people who know how to navigate through challenges. As an individual you encounter problems in your daily life and these problems present you with the occasion to mature your problem-solving skills. Think of how to address a problem before complaining about it. Developing this habit will improve relationships in both your personal and professional life. When probing questions are asked during a job interview to assess your problem-solving skills, you will be equipped to convincingly answer.

- **Conflict Resolution**: Conflict is normal, natural and inevitable. However, there are people who are ignitors, who add fuel to the fire and there are those who find the means to extinguish the flames. If you are the former, you will have problems in any organization you work and will be one who is quickly managed out. The ability to manage differences with colleagues will help to foster good peer relations and an efficient work team. Employers are seeking employees who are emotionally intelligent and mature to handle conflicts and work collaboratively. Develop your ability to reason through conflicts that arise with others, to listen non-judgmentally, and be willing to compromise and accept when you are wrong on any matter.

- **Leadership**: Leadership simply speaks to an individual's ability to guide or direct people to act. Leadership gives you influence over others. Some people have the misconception that leaders in an organization are only the ones with the title of Manager or Supervisor. However, people can lead in any position. When you are confident and knowledgeable, you can influence co-workers to buy into ideas and new initiatives. When you display positive leadership, it is not just seen by your peers but those in authority as well. Your positive leadership abilities can lead to opportunities for upward mobility within an organization. You can develop your leadership skills by accepting opportunities to lead when they come, by volunteering to lead small projects and developing and practicing the art of influencing others.

A lack of, or underdeveloped soft skills, can truly limit your career success. Many employers are keenly looking for and assessing candidates based on their soft skills. Well cultivated soft skills can help you to stand out among several candidates and can determine whether you will soar, plateau or tank as a professional. Invest time and effort to develop these skills.

Chapter Four

Getting Ready for your Future Career

In everything we must be intentional to harvest achievements and rewards. Success lies in preparation as Abraham Lincoln said, "Give me six hours to chop down a tree and I will spend the first four hours sharpening the axe". The work that goes before, determines the probability of success.

Here are five key steps to prepare for your future career.

1. **Know yourself**: Self-knowledge and self-mastery are the foundations on which one builds success. If you know yourself, you know your core strengths and your areas for improvement. Armed with such critical knowledge, you can successfully navigate career paths suited for you. Many people aimlessly go from job to job because they really do not know what lies within them. They have not invested the time in self-excavation to unearth and discover the treasure that is

buried within them. They therefore end up chasing the wind and never catching it. Self-discovering takes deliberate time and effort, but it is worth it. It saves you many years of misery in jobs and careers that bring you no joy, peace and satisfaction.

2. **Research**: Go on a voyage to learn more about your areas of interest. The more you explore and analyse, the sharper your focus will become regarding your career. This is applicable at any age. You may be fifty years old, in an unsatisfying job, doing monotonous work, and worst, among people whose company you do not enjoy. Despite your age and stage start researching what it takes to launch in that area, what are your options for employment or entrepreneurship. Also, research people who are successful in the area and learn some valuable nuggets. Watch podcasts, follow blogs and just soak up all the information you can gather on related subjects. As you journey on your fact-finding exploration, you will be better informed and become more focused about your career interests.

3. **Career Coach:** Career coaches are a great resource to help you figure-out, define or redefine your professional goals. They provide useful guidance to the young graduate, the person desiring to change career paths, the seasoned professional who wants to launch into entrepreneurship or the person seeking to transition to top management. An investment in a good career coach will help you to gain focus and direction, to pilot your professional growth, and keep you targeted on your career goals and accountable.

4. **Ignore the doubting Thomas**: Your career interests and choices do not make sense to some people and they won't hesitate to let you know. That is okay! They are entitled to their opinions but let not their doubt become your doubt. You may be in a "steady" job and decide to switch careers and jump into something very new to you and those around you may naturally be concerned and nervous for you but pursue your passion. If you are an Accountant and want to switch career to do something totally unrelated like Social Work, go after it once you are confident about your

decision. Be flexible with your life and decisions and do not be strangled by the opinions of the Doubting Thomas. Forge ahead to unchartered territories and new terrains to achieve your career dreams and goals.

5. **Be willing to lay the blocks**: A career is not built overnight. It takes planning and preparation. It may also require that you start from foundation and build using one block at a time. This simply means be willing to work your way up and keep expanding your knowledge and skills which will contribute to you being a cut above the rest.

6. **Be open to challenges**: Nothing grows in your comfort zone. Comfort leads to complacency which is the enemy of progress. Be willing to step into a challenge that will allow you to be better and go up higher, to step into a better future. If you only seek opportunities that are familiar, you will not stretch. Your elasticity is dependent on how open you are to challenging yourself.

Chapter Five

Preparing to Hunt

The anxiety that sometimes occur with job searching, keeps some people stuck in meaningless, monotonous, and unfulfilling jobs. There are some who will complain about being unhappy in a job but if an opportunity arises, they are ill-prepared to run with it. Whether an opportunity comes knocking or you wish to go knocking at opportunity's door, preparation is critical. Here are some suggestions to prepare you for whatever opportunities may come your way.

1) **Maintain an up to date resume** – It is common-place for us to just relax when we snag a new job and at that time, we just put away the resume. While the resume remains filed away, we continue working, adding to our accomplishments and skills but those have not been added to our resume. This is the total opposite of what should be done. Even if you have no desire to move-on, you must still capture the information because if an opportunity pops up, you may not have time

to think and accurately craft this critical selling and self-marketing brochure. Ideally, you should update your resume as soon as you get a new job. In short, keep your resume in "ready-to-send" mode.

2) **Keep Studying** – There is so much out there to learn and in your area of work, you should do your best to keep your knowledge current. You can do formal training courses, certifications, and professional development. In addition to completing free online courses from platforms such as Coursera and Alison. As a candidate, you are more impressive and desirable if recruiters see that you have been growing your knowledge. It communicates that you are intrinsically motivated, knowledgeable, progressive and serious about your area of work.

3) **Network** – Building connections is important in any field. By getting to know others in the same field and even other professions increases your visibility, expands your connections, raises your profile, boosts your confidence, and allows you to share ideas and learn from others. When you expand your

professional circle deliberately and strategically, you gain "RECOMMENDATION AGENTS".

Recommendation Agents are people who because they are privy to your work, knowledge, and know your value, as well as your endearing persona, are inclined to speak highly of your professional value and link you with people and opportunities.

When starting to network it may be awkward, but join the professional associations, go to career mingles, training, workshops, and conferences and get to know others. A polite introduction, good chat, intelligent questions, creative suggestion or kind gestures can open you up to people who will be able to advance your career. Take the step and network. Also, when you leave a job remember it is a job and not the people. If you met great, smart and connected people at your former office do your best to nourish the relationship. These people may be part of your past but can also hold the key to your great future.

4) **Stay Motivated** – "If you fell yesterday, stand up today". It is easy to get disheartened when

you keep trying but the doors remain close. Despite how slow you seem to be going or how it may appear that you are taking long to reap success, it is important to maintain a positive attitude and keep motivated. If you lose motivation, your momentum weakens. Apply, reach out to those you know, research the companies that you would love to work with, consistently comb through those job sites and maintain an attitude of expectancy. Do not watch time thinking it is taking too long. Do what time does, keep moving!

5) **LinkedIn™** – Earlier we discussed networking as a means of connecting with others in and outside of your area of expertise. Now let us focus on a key networking tool– LinkedIn™. LinkedIn™ is an awesome online social networking tool for learning and connecting with various professionals across the globe. It is also a good way to showcase "BRAND YOU". You are a brand, and the quality of your brand is determined by your attitude, knowledge, passion and overall competencies. If you are seeking a job, keep your brand updated and relevant. Update your LinkedIn™ profile,

ensure you keep it professional, highlighting your strengths, accomplishments, skills, education and training.

Benefits of having LinkedIn™

A. Excellent for making connections with other professionals. We are now living in a global space and your LinkedIn™ page allows you to connect with other professionals across the globe. It facilitates you sharing your knowledge and perspective but also allows you to gain valuable information from others, participate in discussions and opens you up to job opportunities.

B. **Professional Branding**. As stated before, it allows you to put your personal brand on showcase. When you list your competencies, experiences, accomplishments, training, and education, recruiters can see what you possess and may contact you for possible job opportunities. Also, LinkedIn™ can recommend to you jobs that match the details given in your profile.

C. By being on the platform, you can access the company pages to keep track of job openings. Whenever one comes up that is of interest to you, you may be prompted to apply.

D. LinkedIn™ enables you to remain current on what is happening in your industry, as it is a platform rich with information. If you utilize it well, you will be proactive rather than reactive in your industry. You will be able to swiftly adjust or take advantage of new information, ideas and opportunities. This will aid you in becoming more relevant and marketable.

When preparation and opportunity collide, there is bound to be an explosion of advancement so start preparing to have your explosive moments.

Chapter Six

Choose a Career and not a Job

Many well-intentioned people in our lives encourage us to stay in school, do your work, go to College/University and get a "good job." While we undoubtedly know that such advice was given out of love, concern and wanting the best for us, it was not necessarily the most solid advice. Many of us have followed this encouragement and advice, but it did not culminate in either a fulfilling life, a sense of true accomplishment, or walking in purpose. Rather, it produced a life of monotonous routines, moving to the mundane rhythm of a dull and deficient existence.

Some may cynically call it utopic, but as a living, breathing adult human being, life should be experienced, living out your dreams and aspirations. Use your gifts and talents to their maximum capacity to influence others, effecting positive changes and grasping opportunities. As many millennials put it, living your best life. This best life does not necessarily equate to opulent living (although it is awesome if it does). Rather, it is living a meaningful life which involves engaging in a career that brings satisfaction and a true sense of accomplishment.

Going through the "zombie like" motion of getting up, going to work, doing the tasks and getting paid may for some people produce a comfortable life; however, it does not necessarily mean they feel complete or are even happy doing what they do for a living.

To be confident and content in what you do for a living, more emphasis must be on building careers. From a Strada-Gallup 2017 College Student Survey it was concluded that, *"If students receive career-specific support from their University, they express much greater confidence in their work prospect"*. Thirty-nine percent (39%) of the students who were surveyed expressed confidence that they will graduate with the knowledge and skills they need to be successful in the job market because at least one professor, faculty or staff member initiated a conversation with them about their career options.

What is a job?

A job is a "paid position" of regular employment. A job is merely working and collecting a pay cheque. In the end, when you have a job, you can find yourself going from one company to the next working but not advancing in responsibilities or skills and having no long-term goals or plans. You may also be doing various work in different areas, but the experiences are not value added. A job has one level, one gear – no elevation.

What is a career?

To build a career, you must be focused and have an attitude that says, I want to learn all there is to know in this field. It involves making long-term goals – what can you do now to realize your goals in the future?

To have a career is like climbing a ladder- there are levels to climb and conquer. Each step on the ladder is adding valuable experiences. At one level it could be acquiring new competencies, the level above could be new experiences, the next added interest and as you go higher, you become better and your skills sharper and you become more marketable and confident and importantly, you are more fulfilled as you walk on "career purpose street".

How to Build a Career

1. Know what you are passionate about and good at doing.

2. Acquire the training and education.

3. Learning must be continuous so commit to lifelong learning.

4. Balance work and personal life. Imbalance in this area will cause you to lose focus and passion.

5. Develop values and a sense of purpose.

6. Review, re-engineer or modify your career goals frequently to stay relevant and of course, focused.

Conclusion

In order to give yourself a fighting chance at enjoying life, and living with a sense of purpose and accomplishment, you must enjoy what you are doing. The truth is, we spend most of our adult lives working so it makes sense that you try to have a fulfilling career. On Abraham Maslow's Hierarchy of Needs, the fourth need is Esteem Needs. Maslow classified Esteem Needs into two categories: (a) esteem for oneself, which is acquired through achievements, mastery and independence, and (b) the desire for reputation or respect from others (status, prestige). I dare to say, using Abraham Maslow's five level needs hierarchy that building a meaningful career satisfies one's esteem need. I will also posit that it is imperative for the fifth need of self-actualization, to be realized for a career focused individual, and there must be achievement and reputation – Esteem Need.

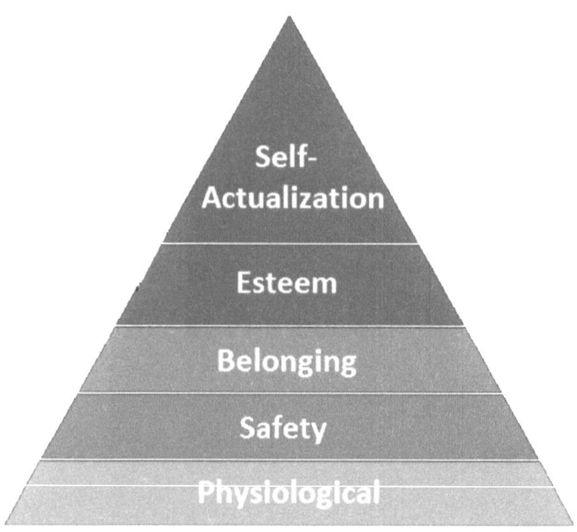

Chapter Seven

Who are your friends?

"He who walks with the wise grows wise, but a companion of fools suffers harms" – Proverbs 13:20. No matter what your age may be, this sound word from the Bible is pertinent and should be heeded.

You have heard the saying, "Your attitude determines your altitude" and this is true. Also true is your circle, your associations, your friendships, those whom you are yoked with, determines your altitude. They are a determining factor in how much or how little you progress. At any age, your circle must be carefully chosen by you because as the Jamaican adage goes, "Show me your friends, and I will tell you who you are".

Tips for choosing the right Friends

1. **Choose friends who are likeminded**. The Bible says, "Can two walk together, except they agree". If you have a progressive, go getter mind-set, you need friends with similar posture because, "iron sharpens iron". Consider having two pieces of iron and rubbing them together. When you rub

them together it causes friction and the metals heat up – the electrons become charged. In the same way, it is important to have likeminded friends because you will both serve to motivate, irritate and fire up each other to achieve goals. Having friends who are not forward thinking or who lack "action orientation" can be sapping to your energy rather than helping to charge you up and motivate you to climb to the mountain top of your ambitions.

2. **Choose purpose partners**. Friends with common goals are your purpose partners, because you push each other, can work on your goals and visions together and encourage each other to continue when the going gets tough. Your purpose partner friends are easy to relate to and can truly empathize and sympathize with you because you are on a similar mission. For example, if you decide to write a book and your friend is also starting his or her journey as an author, you can both provide a support system for each other. You can discuss the challenges being faced and brainstorm over ideas to hurdle barriers and ride out the storms as new authors.

3. **Step up the level of your associations**. It is said that if you want to truly know how the rich live, visit their homes. If you want to upgrade your life, career or business, you must associate with people who are already where you are determined to reach. They can expose you to greater things, be a mentor to you, and keep you focused on where you want to reach, because you are sitting very close to it. In the beginning, you may feel awkward in the presence of these people. You may feel inferior to them, but once you remember the purpose, you will get over all those feelings or manage those feelings of insecurity. Make the best of every moment you have with "higher level crew".

4. **Choose friends who can assist you in your areas of deficiency.** Let us face it, we are not all good at everything. The truth is that there are some things at which we are just not good at doing! Having friends who are strong in your areas of weakness is phenomenal. If you are not prideful, you are able to seek help from your friends to develop your competencies in your specific areas of deficiencies. You may also be able to offer support to them in areas that they need to develop. *"Blind cannot lead the blind"*.

5. **Choose friends that stretch you**. An elastic band that is never stretched is unable to hold as many things as one that has gone under the pressure of prior stretching. When you have friends that hold you accountable, that demand that you do more and reach higher, they push you to become a better version of yourself, and you will either run from those friendships or stretch as they demand. When you stretch yourself, you will be happy with yourself for all you achieve.

6. **Choose friends that celebrate your successes**. As the saying goes, *"Some people or friends may want to see you do good, but not better than them"*. True friends celebrate each other's successes, milestones and accomplishments. They hold the banner and genuinely say congratulations. When choosing friends, be careful and watchful of their reactions to your successes. Know who you can keep close and who to keep at a distance. Consider the example of the greatest teacher – Jesus Christ. He had twelve disciples yet three of them; Peter, James and John were in his inner circle. When Jesus was being transfigured on the Mountain, He did not allow all to see just Peter, James & John (Matthew

17: 1-8). Also, when He went to the Garden of Gethsemane, He took the same three to help Him bear the burden as He prayed before His betrayal by Judas and His crucifixion (Mark 14:32-50). It is also wise to manage your expectations of others. We are all fallible and thus prone to offend. So do not be too harsh with others just be intuitive and particular in choosing your inner-circle.

Exercise.

Considering the nuggets above, think of your three, your inner circle; the people who you would take to Mount of Transfiguration & Garden of Gethsemane. Also, state the qualities you have seen in them that makes them your inner circle.

Name	Reason for Choosing

Chapter Eight

Do not live in a state of someday

Some people live their best lives in their imagination. In their land of imagination, there is a never-ending flow of milk and honey but sadly in reality, many are still sucking on sour grapes and eating unripen fruits. The reason for this overflow in imagination and suffering or starvation in reality is INCAPACITATION BY FEAR. They fail to jump into that amazing life because they live their lives shackled by "limited resources". They live safely "within their means" and continuously dream of someday.

How do you jump out of the someday state to "ACTION STATE?"

1. ***Write down the illustrious vision/what you imagine your life to be.*** In the bible, Habakkuk 2:2 the Word says, "Write the vision, and make it plain upon tablets that he may run that readeth it". When you write down what you imagine, it is the first step in making it a reality. You can put perspective on it. Seeing your vision or imagination in writing ignites the fire within and propels you to action.

2. ***Prepare a roadmap.*** Before this era of GPS, people relied on physical roadmaps. The roadmaps provide clear paths and milestones that you would follow to get from one point to another. If you travelled to unknown cities and to the countryside with a roadmap and without having any idea of which roads to take, you would likely end up lost, frustrated and delayed in getting to your destination. In the same way coasting through life without a strategic roadmap, will cause you to take many off-paths down dead-end streets and waste precious time. Preparing a life roadmap defines and refines your goals and desired outcomes for the ventures you will embark on in your life. It breaks down major steps and milestones you will take to achieve your visions and goals.

3. ***Jump without worrying where your feet will land***. The fear of the unknown can be crippling because we have been conditioned to walk by EYESIGHT and not INSIGHT. Eyesight in this context can be debilitating because we are so focused on looking out for stumbling blocks that we lose the perspective of the horizon

(the big picture). Like walking with blinders, there is no peripheral sight. Conversely, when you walk by insight, you move instinctively. You will jump, having the confidence that you will land on safe ground. This confidence comes from your assurance that your vision and roadmap are clear and above all, you are confident in self.

4. ***Be relentless and consistent***. Operate in a never-ending pursuit of better. When you are relentless, you are focused, determined and apply consistent effort and energy towards achieving your someday. At different times and stages in your life, different goals should be your focus. This simply speaks to the maturity of your desires. The maturity results not just from age but from changes in life circumstances. For example, deciding to start a family causes you to forgo singular focused mind-set to family whether it be a spouse, a child or both.

For each milestone or phase in life there must be some accomplishment that you fix your mind on achieving. Without having a vision, you simply drift, wandering aimlessly through the forests of life with life happening to you. If this is an example of your current situation, it is time to wake up to the reality that you are merely existing.

Being relentless and consistent does not guarantee a smooth path. In fact, such belief is idealistic and euphoric. However, despite the challenges that may be presented, as you pursue to live your someday, the climbs, falls, bruises and scars are worth the exhilaration you get from a feeling of accomplishment. **STOP IMAGINING AND START LIVING!**

The exercise on the next page will help you to begin to move from the "someday" state to action state. In completing this exercise, be purposeful, honest with yourself and focused. Consider all the elements (people, resources, training etc.) you will need to make your goals a reality and by when you will need to have them. A goal must be SMART – **S**pecific, **M**easurable, **A**ttainable, **R**elevant and **T**ime-bound.

AWAKE Exercise: Write the vision and make it plain.

What are the top three goals you wish to accomplish within the year (be specific)?

#	Goals	Target Date to Achieve	Tasks to Accomplish
1			
2			
3			

After completing this exercise, create your vision board.

A vision Board is a collage of images representing your goals. Its purposes are to:

- Help you to meditate on your life and future

- Narrow your focus on your goals

- Keeps you inspired to achieve the goals

- Keeps you accountable

- Propels you to AWAKE, stop dreaming and start living

Chapter Nine

You better tear those muscles!

If you have lived a sedentary life, and decide to embark on an exercise program, initially you feel soreness and aches all over.

Sometimes simple actions such as walking and sitting become so difficult because of the tension in your muscles from the workout. At other times the intensity of the pain makes you want to just quit. But, when you keep at it, the pain diminishes, and you see the results.

How to build muscles

I am no expert in body building or the anatomy of the body, but I will explain from my layman understanding. After you work-out, your body repairs or replaces damaged muscle fibres by fusing them together to form new muscle protein strands, which are called myofibrils. The repaired myofibrils increase in thickness and number to create muscle growth. Muscle growth occurs after muscles have been broken-down. For this growth to occur, one must force their muscles to adapt by creating stress different and greater than the previous threshold your body had already adapted to. Essentially, you must increase the intensity of pressure, lift heavier weights, do more leg lifts, more pushups and overall, push and go harder than the day before. You must damage more muscle fibres and push your muscles to fatigue then, you get that "ripped" body you lustfully desired.

How is this applicable to life or everyday living?

In the same way that our bodies must undergo some pressure, stretching and stressing to get into shape, our lives also need to go through the rigour to achieve goals and aspirations. Attaining goals and walking in purpose, are not achieved by "microwave living". There is no quickie for long and lasting success. The right amount of pressure must be applied. Consider squeezing an orange, if you hold it and apply little pressure to it, the juice flow will trickle; however, when you hold it tightly and apply the necessary pressure, the juice sacs will explode with flowing orange juice. Likewise, to juice your purpose and make the best of opportunities in life, pressure must be applied.

In pursuing any career, there is a time that you must diligently study. To be a lawyer, it takes approximately five years, or to become a doctor - seven years. For each career, you must invest time in studying. If you quit before finishing the prescribed number of years, it does not matter what you learnt in relation to the career, you cannot claim it as your profession. A mechanic, carpenter or mason must spend time honing their skills. They must subject themselves to the tutelage of others in the trade, be diligent apprentices and train to master their skills. An unskilled craftsman will not survive in his trade because he will not be recommended for jobs.

Nothing grows and flourishes in the land of too comfortable. When you are too comfortable, you are not provoked to do more or to be more.

As physiology and nature has taught us, regeneration, rejuvenation, and outpour occur after we stretch beyond our norm and apply some pressure to ourselves. If you want to be successful in any career and in life in general, you must be consistent with your efforts, push hard, learn more, sleep less, give up some leisure time, and most importantly, commit to all you are doing. As you plug in and keep at it, you will realize that as you get closer to your goals, it gets easier. You begin to see results, feel better, and you feel a sense of pride for having stayed the course.

Un-stretched Muscles	Execution plan to tear and build the muscles	Re-construction Commencement Date

Conclusion

After consistent grueling work-out, muscles regenerate and grow. In the same way your success and reward will come after you push beyond yourself.

GO TEAR YOUR MUSCLES!

"BODY-BUILDER" EXERCISE

Consider the aspects of your life that are like unused or un-stretched muscles. Write them down and also write how you plan to tear and build them. You must also have a target time so state when you intend to start.

Now, to hold yourself accountable, get an accountability partner who you know will do just that – keep you accountable.

Chapter Ten

Faith it until you Make It!

"Now faith is the substance of things hoped for, the evidence of things not seen" Hebrews 11:1

There are many things that people desire in life but sometimes just do not see how it is all going to happen. Generally there are two reactions to this dilemma:-

1. People give up – they just say, "Forget about it, it is out of my reach."

2. Some spring into action. They begin to plan and strategize how to make it possible – what do I need to do? Who do I need to meet? Where do I need to go to get this desire to be realized?

The latter group are the ones with NOW FAITH – Faith in action. They have a thought, a goal, a desire, a vision and they believe in it. They have faith and move towards achieving the goal. This "Now Faith" is not just in reference to tangible achievements.

Many people have a vision of who they want to become, the way they wish to be, the attributes they wish to develop. To embody the desired attributes, you must Faith It (Act it) until you become it. Sometime ago I listened to a Youtuber who shared how she became who she is now. She recounted that she had a vision of the lady she aspired to be, and she took that vision and began her transformation. She began to dress like the person, talk like the person, went where the person would go, read the books the person would read and embodied the essence of the lady she longed to become. By her continuous deliberate actions, she began to shed the attitudes and behaviours she had, and embraced the character, behaviours and attributes of the lady she envisioned to exemplify. Congruence occurred between who she envisioned and who she became. She "Faithed It", until she became it.

Why is this story so powerful? Many people are fed up with their station or position in life, the person they are, that is, the attitudes they display and want to be better. However, they stay stuck because of the belief that God made them that way so they cannot change. This is a lie. God's plan for you are good. The Word of God says, "For I know the plans I have for you, declares the Lord, plans to prosper you and not to harm you, plans to give you hope and a future" – Jeremiah 29:11.

God wants us to be the best version of ourselves, not a carbon of someone else.

Exercise: Write down what attributes you would like to develop, and your action plan to develop them. Make everything time bound and hold yourself accountable.

Chapter Eleven

Swimming with the sharks

Not many people would knowingly get into a shark infested water. Only the extremely adventurous or crazy would do so. Marine Biologist or Deep-Sea Divers hunting in the name of science, for artefacts, riches and even fame, go into the deep blue sea knowing the danger that lies beneath. In order to increase their likelihood of coming out alive, they suit-up in the right gears, they have a team with an evacuation plan and importantly, they mentally prepare for the unknown.

Venturing in a new job, new office environment may be likened to the treacherous unknown. You may from the outside hear all the glowing reports about the company's successes and bright future but, because you have never worked in that company, you have no idea what it is really like. For many people, they walk into the new environment ill-prepared for the possible drama and office politics that awaits. But just as how you prepared for and aced the interview, you can prepare to navigate the possible "shark infested" office and maneuver despite office politics.

<u>**What is Office Politics?**</u>

Office Politics is described in the Miriam-Webster's Dictionary as the activities, attitudes, or behaviours that are used to get or keep power or advantage within a business or company. This can be used in a good or bad way. Where it is used negatively and involves backbiting, double-crossing, side conversations and gossiping, this kind of environment can be crippling if you do not have a game plan to deal with it.

How to combat the drama?

1. **Know yourself**. Own your value and never doubt what you bring to the company. By doing this, you are developing the confidence and strong sense of self and purpose you must have to hold your own amidst the toxicity and negativity.

2. **Be a Star Player**. When you show that you are a star, you are set apart from the rest. Your upper management will see your value and will give you the room and autonomy to do your work. This builds your immunity. As a star player, people respect you just because of the work you do.

3. **Manage the tsunami**. Know what arguments you engage in. A lack of conflict does not say all is well, so engage in conflict where necessary. However, the conflict must never be on a personal level rather, it must be about professional work-related matters. For example, if a colleague, manager or co-worker wants to argue with you about what they perceive to be a "bad look" that you gave them or you walking pass them and perhaps brushing them unintentionally or just about anything from politics to religion, respectfully excuse yourself from that unproductive conflict. You can politely apologize to them for what they perceived. Careful not to say, "I am sorry for…"; rather, you may say "I am sorry you are of the belief that I did XYZ." Say nothing while they rant and then politely excuse yourself without saying another word. Now on the professional side, conflict is healthy and necessary. You must be willing to defend a decision, speak with colleagues about tardiness in meeting deadlines, inefficiency in handling a project. Matters that will impact the efficiency of the company, your deportment or team must be

dealt with and not ignored. But keep the discussions centered on the issues not people.

4. **Manage your work friendships**. The sharks and gossipmongers are not hard to spot. Once you identify them, you develop a strategy on how to manage your interactions. Keep conversations with them centered on business – STRICTLY PROFESSIONAL. If you are around them and they begin to gossip, politely excuse yourself. This will send a clear message that you are not into that discussion. Additionally, never interact with them socially outside of the office. This is for two reasons; you do not want others to begin associating you as a close friend or confidant of the shark or gossipmongers and secondly you do not want whatever you may say or do on your private time to become office business. They are quick to take weekend discussions back to the office.

5. **Set yourself apart**. Hone your craft and become exceptional at your area, to develop a good reputation. Colleagues, managers and directors will respect you for that value you add to the work environment.

While you must be mindful of negative office politics, be assured it can be used for good. Once you understand the power plays within any company, you are well on your way to navigate effective. Use office politics to:

1. **Increase your knowledge base**. From the wielding of power that you may see, you will get to know the people who have knowledge from which you can benefit and grow. So, seek audience with them with the clear focus on learning about the business. This will help you to increase your value as well as build professional relationships.

2. **Use it to develop your people skills** or as my Bishop Courtney McLean says, "People Mastery". Study people around you, learn how to communicate with all personality types and how to say things best and know what to say. It is best to use wisdom and not reveal all that is in your heart.

3. **Allow office politics to also build your character and your integrity**. Know what you stand for, what your values are and stick to them uncompromisingly. People may try to

pull you in tsunamis that do not concern you but as you develop your character and integrity, you will know how to diplomatically resist.

Conclusion

My mother has often says, "I can go to hell and live with the devil". She is basically saying that she knows how to navigate her way around difficult people and situations and be just fine. If you follow the guidelines given above, you too can live or work with the "devil" and no doubt swim in shark infested water and remain untainted and unbitten. Also, you can be a stellar example right there.

Chapter Twelve

How to know if this is YOUR job

In this very competitive labour market, it can be a real hustle to land a job out of the numerous candidates vying for the one position.

The eagerness to gain employment may cause your judgment to be murky and result in you ignoring glaring warning signs that the job and the company are not a fit for you. When you ignore the warning signals, you find yourself in situations that lead to feelings of regret, depression, and unfulfillment. It also often causes underperformance due to being woefully uncomfortable in the new job and company.

While no job or organization is perfect, there are some situations that can be avoided if we just pay attention to the clues. The truth is that the signs are often hidden in plain sight and are not hard to see.

Warning Signs

1. ***The job was being advertised for a long time.***
   This often says, they cannot find anyone who

is willing to take it. Ask yourself why this is so. While there are some jobs that require some special skills and it may be difficult to recruit, these are exceptions. It is quite likely that is not the reason for the long advertising period.

2. ***The turnover for the position is high.*** This is self-explanatory, if the holders of the position keep leaving that is a red flag. The job may be a highly stressful position, the manager may be difficult to get along with, poor work and leisure life balance, lack of support from company leadership and ethical issues with the company.

3. ***Desperate or Pushy Recruiter.*** An overly pushy recruiter or Human Resources Manager should cause one to stop and think. I can say that I have in the past learnt a personal lesson from this one. Be very aware.

4. **The interviewer fumbles to respond to your questions about the company, its culture and the reason for the position being vacant.** It could be that he or she is ill prepared for the questions you are posing as well as, he or she

may be trying to avoid the question. Either way it is not a good sign.

5. **The job poses an ethical dilemma**. Is there need for more to be said about this? I think NOT! If the job is one in which you may likely have to do or say things that conflict with your morals, ethical principles and values then you must politely reject it!

6. **There is incongruence between your career objectives and the job**. If the job is not advancing your career objectives and you are serious about your future goals, it is a clear indication that it is not the job for you. The job may be financially lucrative but stifling professionally. Have a checklist of what the job must offer to align with your objectives and check if the job lines up. You cannot fit a square peg into a round hole.

Conclusion

There is a saying, *"only fools rush in"* and for those of us who are Christians we know the Bible says, *"Commit to the Lord whatever you do, and He will establish your plans"* – Proverbs 16 vs 3. Never be too hasty to accept a job. Yes, there are many candidates waiting to snatch the opportunity but do your due diligence.

While no job is a "ride in the park" make sure both the job and the company that is, its culture and value systems are a match for you. Otherwise being hasty and ignoring the warnings, will leave you in deep regret and anguish.

Chapter Thirteen

Make your last waltz your best waltz

No matter how many good performances you have had, you are always remembered by your last "Act".

Oftentimes, people bring their A-game when they start a new job. They are on their best behaviour, go above and beyond the call of duty by showing eagerness to learn and just "do the most". Fast forward to when they have decided to leave the organization and the script changes. Unfortunately, there are many people from clerical to managerial levels, who go on cruise control after they tender their resignations and sometimes before, because they know the resignation is coming. They take up a seat in the departure lounge and all the "A" leaves their game. Work falls off, deadlines not met and generally a nonchalant "I don't care" attitude. My experiences as a Human Resource Practitioner has been that some deliberately leave a mess of their portfolio thus making it difficult for the next person in the role to hit the ground running.

<u>**True horror story**</u>

A friend of mine has had the misfortune of working in organizations where the predecessor left the Human Resources portfolio in a mess. In one instance, she went to work with a company where the Human Resources Manager left under disgraceful circumstances; he flipped out and used expletives to employees during a heated argument. However, before taking his leave of the company, he deleted all Human Resources Policies and Procedures, and all other related Human Resources documents. Unfortunately, there were no backups. This resulted in her starting from scratch to rebuild the Human Resource Department.

The spiteful act of that former Human Resources Manager spoke volumes about his character. It certainly would make it difficult for him to get a recommendation from that company, despite how brilliantly he worked prior to his uncouth display and reprehensible act.

Despite how frustrated you may get working with an organization, for as long as you are employed there, do the job for which you were hired. The level of your performance should not plummet because you are separating from a company.

Bridges (relationships) take time to be established so let it count for something. When you burn bridges behind you, remember there is no going back. Also be mindful that within the business circle, people are connected so even if you have no intention or desire to return to the company, they may know people with whom you will later socialize or work with and a bad reputation can keep you from advancing.

During your last months or weeks at a company, you should do the following:

1. Complete all outstanding matters.

2. Ensure you tidy up all files; online or physical.

3. Update your manager on the status of your desk.

4. If there are upcoming matters that will require attention when you leave, notify the relevant colleagues who will need to assist in handling them and leave some guidance or instruction.

5. Go the extra-mile in all areas.

6. BE EXTRA – Leave a roadmap for the incumbent and be open to reach out and assist the person if you can. This will just make

their transition into the company much easier. Also, if you can, reach out and assist in their training. Do unto others as you would like done unto you.

Conclusion

When you step on that dance floor for your last dance, ensure your posture and steps are on point as you waltz. People will recall the final performance much better than they will the first.

CLEAN UP YOUR **ACT!**

Action:

- What you do

Consequences:

- What happens as a result of your actions

Thoughts:

- The thoughts that precede your actions, and those which are generated by your actions and its consequences

Chapter Fourteen

Go the 40th time!

In Jamaican vernacular, "Mi dun, mi give up, it too hard!" Translation: "I am over this, I am giving up, it is too hard for me!" Does all that sound familiar? Perhaps it does, because we have all said those words at some point. Be encouraged, because inspiration is all around us to let us know that we can win, if we push and keep hope alive.

Figure 1 - WD40 is the registered trademark of WD Manufacturing Company

The beloved "all purpose" **WD-40®**, would not have existed if its creator Norm Larsen had given up on his 39th try and failure at the formula. Norm Larsen was determined to perfect his Water Displacement formula and so he did, on the 40th try! He developed **WD-40®** in 1953 and today, the company is valued at over US$1.3 billion dollars.

The product is credited with over 2000 uses from the sober and sensible, to the bizarre and wacky, such as to remove a naked burglar trapped in an air conditioning vent.

Moral of the Story - To win at life, it takes an attitude of "stick-to-itiveness". We must tenaciously reach for our goals; changing tactics when we need to, but never dimming the light on the goal. Whatever your personal goals, believe that you can and will achieve them and be relentless in your pursuit.

My Final Words

The process of writing this book, (which I pray will be a blessing to you) required the investment of my time, talents and trust.

Time: To write this book required research, moments of solitude, hours with my pen and notebook and hours being at one with my laptop. Time is the interlock of preparation and success. You must spend time preparing to yield success.

Talents: I thank God for the gift of writing. We have all been gifted with abilities and skills that have been divinely planted in us to make room for us and bring us before great men (Proverbs 18:16). If I did not take this literary journey, I would not have massaged, matured and manifested my talent. Whatever we do not use, we ultimately will lose.

Trust: Yes Trust. At times, we believe in the potential and abilities of others but struggle to believe in ourselves. Many people live a life looking at the accomplishment of others and dreaming of someday not because they are lazy, but because they have not developed Trust in themselves. I trusted myself to be able to utilize my God given ability to write. I trusted myself by believing that I have knowledge to share, I trusted myself to take a chance on me, and this took an investment of self-belief.

My parting words to you are, know you have talents, you have much to offer any corporation you choose to bless with your talents. But to hone your talent, you must be willing to put in the work by investing your time in learning new skills, acquiring knowledge, and creating and polishing your best self to present to others. But talent and time without trust or Belief in self will be wasted. I dare you to just Trust that you are a valuable resource, you are an asset to any organization, you are born to impact, and you are born to soar.

Succeed on purpose!

About Stacy-Ann M. Nelson

Stacy-Ann M. Nelson is a Human Resource professional with over ten years' experience. Throughout her career, she has a proven track record of being a transformational Human Resource leader, who is keen on uncovering inefficiencies, and developing practical solutions to mitigate against inadequacies to create a high performing organization, with motivated employees. Pursuing a B.A Degree in Psychology, and a MSc. in Human Resource Development, are testaments of her keen interest in the development of the human resource.

She has dedicated her life to the service of others. For eight years, she invested her time in helping children in need of Care and Protection, mending broken families and advancing the lives of people, through her work as a Children's Officer (Social Worker) and Manager of a residential child care facility.

She has a passion for aiding others to truly be their best selves and live life owning every day, being accountable to self, going after better, and never settling for mediocre. As a Christian, she firmly believes that all were created by God with divine purpose, and to truly be fulfilled, purpose must be discovered and lived. To be an authentic Ambassador of her message, Stacy-Ann embarked on her journey as an author and this book is the fruit.

Connect with the author

 stacyannmnelson@gmail.com

 www.instagram.com/stacyspeakstruths

 www.linkedin.com/in/stacy-ann-nelson